neighborhoods in nature™

Let's Take a
Field Trip to an
Ant Colony

Kathy Furgang

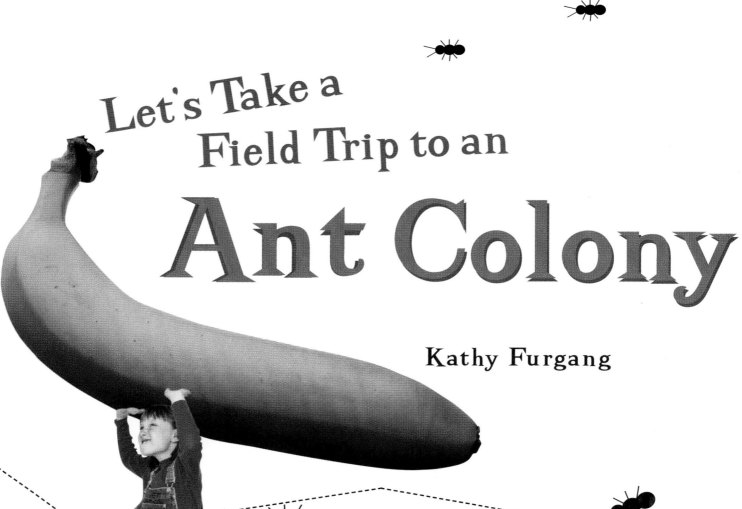

The Rosen Publishing Group's
PowerKids Press™
New York

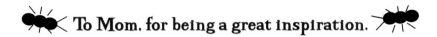 **To Mom, for being a great inspiration.**

Published in 2000 by The Rosen Publishing Group, Inc.
29 East 21st Street, New York, NY 10010

Photo Credits: p. 4 © CORBIS/Bettman; p. 7 © Animals, Animals; p. 8 © Animals, Animals, © CORBIS/Bettman, p. 11 © Animals, Animals, © CORBIS/Bettman, © Minden Pictures; p. 12 © CORBIS/Bettman; p. 15 Animals, Animals; p. 16 © CORBIS/Bettman; p. 19 © Archive Photos, © CORBIS/Bettman; p. 20 © CORBIS/Bettman, p. 20 © CORBIS/Bettman, p. 22–23 © Uncle Milton Industries.

First Edition

Book Design: Felicity Erwin

Furgang, Kathy.
    Let's take a field trip to an ant colony / by Kathy Furgang.
        p.   cm. — (Neighborhoods in nature)
    Includes index.
    Summary: An introduction to ant society, discussing roles and duties of individual ants, the creation of a nest, the anatomy of an ant, and the relationship of these insects to humans.
    ISBN 0-8239-5444-7 (lib. bdg.)
    1. Ants—Juvenile literature. 2. Insect societies—Juvenile literature. [1. Ants. 2. Insect societies.] I. Title. II. Series: Furgang, Kathy. Neighborhoods in nature.
    QL568.F7F87 1999
    595.79'6—dc21
                                                                        98-52906
                                                                        CIP
                                                                        AC

Manufactured in the United States of America

Contents

What Is ?

◀ *Ants live and work around the world except for places that have very cold climates.*

an Ant Colony?

Ants stay together in large groups. A group of ants is called an ant colony. Colonies can have hundreds or millions of ants living in them. Insects that live and work together are **social insects**.

An ant colony is a big **community**. Ants spend most of their time looking for enough food to feed the colony. They also spend time in their homes which are called **nests**. They take care of their nests and store food there. They use the food to feed their baby ants. Ants work hard to meet the needs of their colony.

Making a Home

Ants can make their homes almost anywhere. Their nests are often dug into sand or dirt. Ants dig down into the ground and make **chambers**, or rooms, that connect to each other by hallways. Each chamber has a special purpose in the colony. Some chambers are for resting and sleeping, some are used to store food, and others are used as rooms for baby ants. As a colony grows, ants build more chambers and tunnels to meet the needs of the growing community.

Ants can build their nests in the ground, ▶
in logs, in trees, and even in houses.

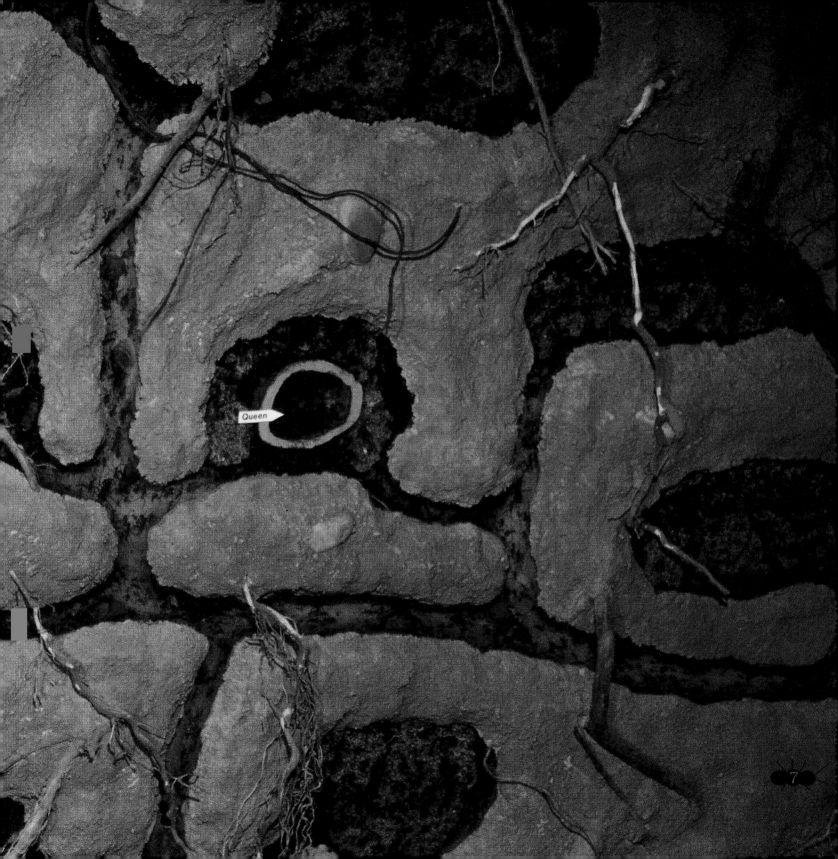

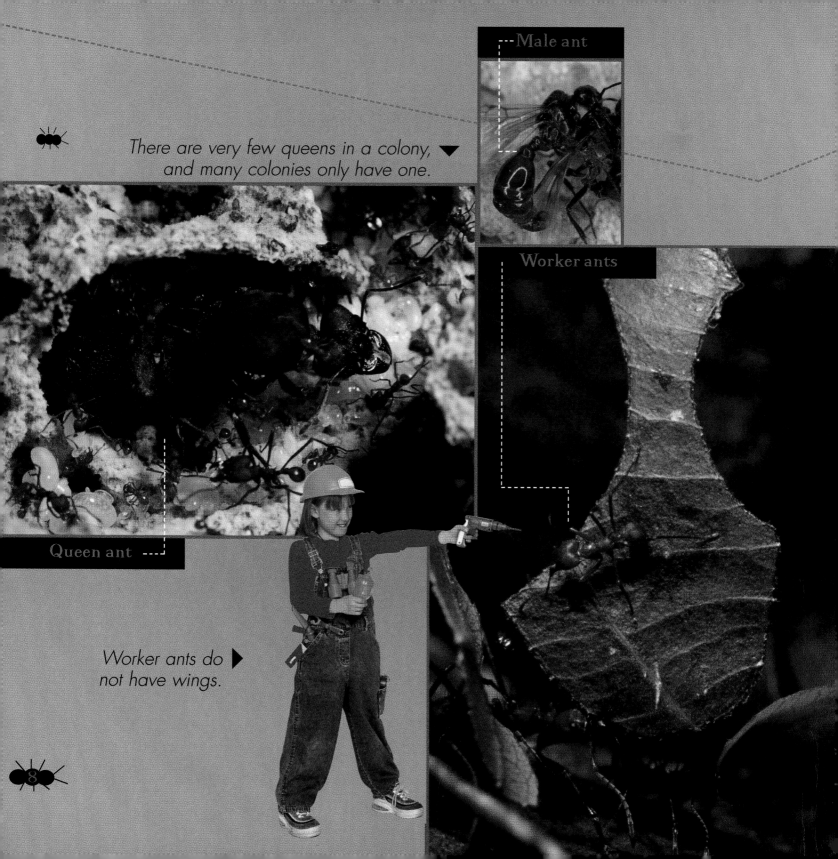

*There are very few queens in a colony, ▼
and many colonies only have one.*

Male ant

Worker ants

Queen ant ---

*Worker ants do ▶
not have wings.*

8

Each Ant Has a Job to Do

Every colony is made up of three kinds of ants. The **queen ant** usually starts the colony and makes it grow by laying eggs and producing more ants. To do this she flies off with thousands of **male ants**. Male ants and the queen are the only ants that have wings. The males join together, or **mate**, with her while flying. This is the male ant's only job. Soon after the males mate with the queen, they die.

The other females in a colony are called **worker ants**. They build the nest, find food for the colony, care for the young, and fight enemies.

There Are Many Kinds of Ants

All ants can be divided into six large groups. Each group is named after the kind of work it does best.

Harvester ants collect and store seeds. **Army ants** are best at hunting other insects. **Honey ants** take honey from other insects and store it in their nests. **Slave makers** attack other ant nests and steal eggs so they can raise more ants to work in their own colony. **Fungus growers** raise different kinds of **molds** so they can have enough food for the ants in their community to share. **Dairying ants** get their food by sucking on a sweet liquid called honeydew.

All of these different kinds of ants live in North America. Many ▶ *of them live in Asia, Europe, South America, and Africa.*

Harvester ants

Army ants

Honey ants

Slave makers

Fungus Grower ant

Dairying ants

Amazing Ants

There are more ants in the world than any other living creature. Ants are very strong and work hard. They can lift things that are 10 to 50 times the weight of their own bodies! Ants can carry leaves, dead insects, garbage, and anything else they want to eat.

Every ant has two long feelers called **antennae** attached to its head. Tiny hairs on the antennae allow the ants to smell, touch, taste, and hear. Ants tap the ground with their antennae to smell the air and other things around them. Ants use their feelers to help them find the things they collect as food. They also use their feelers to help them taste their food before they eat it.

The ants' antennae are almost always moving. These ▶ *feelers help ants smell and hear nearby enemies.*

Excellent Hunters

Ants are great hunters. Although they are small, they capture and kill insects that are much larger than themselves. Ants hunt in large numbers. Between 10,000 to 100,000 ants travel together to find food or to hunt enemies. Ants have been known to eat dead animals, such as snakes and even horses, in a matter of hours. When the ants are finished feasting, only the skeleton of their meal is left. These hunting trips last for about 17 days. Ants then return home to rest for about 20 days and eat food they have stored in the nest.

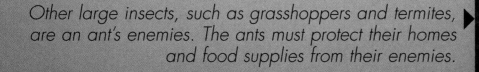

Other large insects, such as grasshoppers and termites, are an ant's enemies. The ants must protect their homes and food supplies from their enemies.

▲ Ants that find their way into houses can live for a long time on small crumbs left behind a cabinet, stove, or on the floor. These ants enjoy some honey that spilled on someone's kitchen floor.

16

Very Successful
Insects

Ants' bodies are very good at **adapting**, or changing, to different temperatures and conditions. Ants do not mind the changes in temperature from season to season. Ants are also successful because they are so small. The ants' small size allows them to explore areas that other animals and insects cannot reach. They can crawl into small cracks in trees or under the ground to find food. Scientists who study insects say that ants can eat almost anything. A colony of ants can march into a garbage can, pick out food that humans have thrown out, and feed the ants in their colony with it.

What Do Ants Mean to Us?

Ants are both helpful and hurtful to humans. They can be very helpful to farmers by keeping the soil rich and **fertile**. When ants travel in and out of the ground it moves the soil and allows rainwater to soak in more easily, which helps plants grow.

Ants can kill plants too, which means trouble for people who grow gardens. Sometimes ants eat plants or vegetables faster than they can grow. This makes the plants or vegetables die.

Most of the time, however, humans walk right by ants and hardly notice them at all.

Humans know ants best as unwanted guests at picnics. ▶

18

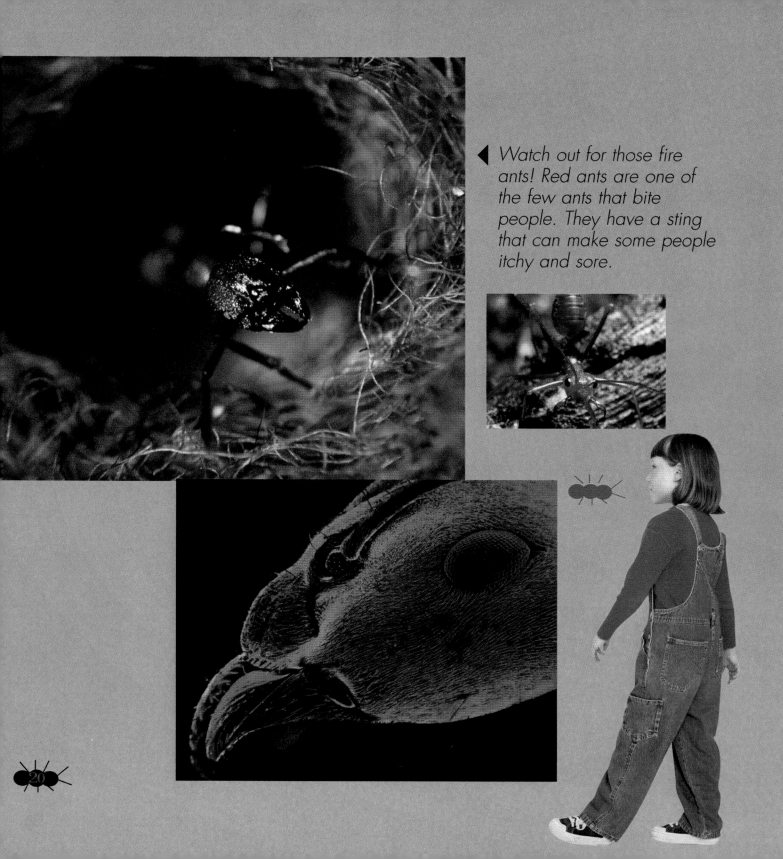

Watch out for those fire ants! Red ants are one of the few ants that bite people. They have a sting that can make some people itchy and sore.

20

Studying Ants

Most ants are dark colors such as black, brown, or rust, but ants come in other colors, too. Some ants are green, purple, blue, or yellow. Different colored ants have been found all around the world. In each colony though, you will find ants that are all the same color.

How long do ants live? Scientists who study ants have found that male ants live only a few weeks or months. Female worker ants can live from a year to five years. The queen lives the longest of all. She can live up to 20 years!

Making Your Own Ant Colony

You can be a scientist by making an ant colony. With an adult's help, put a sealed jar inside a larger, clear jar. The small jar keeps the sand near the glass so it's easy to watch the ants. Fill the large jar with sand and ants. Keep the top of the sand wet by placing a damp towel over it. Feed the ants fruit. Cover the jar with black paper for a week so the ants can dig tunnels. When you remove the paper, you'll see the cool things these creatures can do.

Web Sites

You can learn more about ants and ant colonies at these Web sites:
http://www.entsoc.org/education/edfarm.htm
http://ezra.mts.jhu.edu/~naomi/insects/ants.html

ANT FARM

Glossary

adapting (uh-DAP-ting) Changing to fit in with new conditions.

antennae (an-TEH-nee) Two long feelers attached to the front of an ant's head that allow it to touch, taste, hear, and smell.

army ants (AR-mee ANTS) Ants that hunt and fight other insects.

chambers (CHAYM-burz) Rooms in an ant colony.

community (kuh-MYOO-nih-tee) A group of people or animals that share things and help care for one another.

dairying ants (DAYR-ee-ing ANTS) Ants that get their food by sucking on a sweet liquid called honeydew.

fertile (FUR-tul) Good for making and growing things.

fungus growers (FUN-gis GRO-wurz) Ants that grow and eat molds.

harvester ants (HAR-vis-tur ANTS) Ants that collect and store seeds.

honey ants (HUH-nee ANTS) Ants that gather and store honey.

male ants (MAYL ANTS) Ants with wings that mate with the queen ant.

mate (MAYT) When a male and female join together to make babies.

molds (MOLDZ) Fuzzy plants that grow on something that is kept in a damp, warm place.

nests (NESTZ) Homes that ants make by digging in the ground or into small spaces in trees.

queen ant (KWEEN ANT) The most important ant in a colony and the mother to most of the other ants.

slave makers (SLAYV MAY-kurz) Ants that attack other nests and take eggs of unborn ants.

social insects (SO-shul IN-sekts) Insects that live and work together in groups.

worker ants (WUR-kur ANTS) Female ants in a colony.

Index